The Cats of Laughing Thunder in

Fritz's Weather Favorites

S. S. Curtis

In memory of my parents Jack and Joan

Contents

Chapter 1 – Introduction

I want everyone to love meteorology as much as I do. So I asked S. S. Curtis to write this book—with my expert help, of course. Read on for information about my favorite weather topics. Arctic inversion, blizzard, dust devil, sun dog, thundersnow, tornado, and more – let's talk about them all!

Chapter 2 – Arctic Inversion

Arctic inversions are super interesting – I've even written a song about them!

Scientists are still studying inversions over the Arctic. Scientists list many reasons for an Arctic inversion. The two main reasons are:

Radiation imbalance. During the Arctic winter, solar radiation—or heat from the sun—doesn't reach the ground. The ground does continue to send off 'longwave radiation' or heat. This can cause more heat to come from the earth than does from the sun. In this imbalance, the ground surface cools while the air remains warm.

Warm air advection. For much of the year, the Arctic ground surface is cool. When warm air moves in, the warmer air can trap the cooler air. This causes an arctic inversion where cold air is trapped next to the ground.

Chapter 3 – Aurora Borealis

The Aurora Borealis is a tremendous light show in the sky!

It is caused when particles from the sun collide with the earth's oxygen. The lights are seen around the North and South Poles.

When the lights are seen in the northern hemisphere, they are called "Aurora Borealis."

When the lights appear in the southern hemisphere, they are called "Aurora Australis."

Scientists believe auroras are mirror-like images. While green is the most common color, other colors such as yellow, red, blue, and violet are sometimes seen.

The color differences are because of the type of gas particles colliding.

The best place to watch an Aurora is as close to the earth's poles as you can get!

Chapter 4 – Blizzard

Snowstorms happen in many areas, but blizzards are rare!

To be called a blizzard, a snowstorm must have:

A large amount of snowfall,

Winds blowing faster than 35 miles-per-hour,

And less than a quarter-mile visibility—the distance you can see.

These conditions must last longer than three hours

During a snowstorm, temperatures fall below zero. This is when frostbite may happen – stay safe and dress warmly.

In the United States, blizzards happen in the Plains states, the Midwestern states, the Northeastern states, and any states with mountain tops—anywhere that gets snow.

A famous blizzard happened in the Midwest on November 11, 1940—the Armistice Day Blizzard. Many children went to school that day in short-sleeve shirts, as the day was unseasonably warm. Mistress Josheka's grandfather Jack was one of those children.

But in the middle of the day, temperatures dropped sharply. An intense low pressure system moved in, pulling moisture from the Gulf of Mexico and pulling cold air from the Arctic.

The result was a raging blizzard that dropped

up to 27 inches of snow, and had winds up to 80 miles per hour.

As soon as the blizzard started, Jack's father got in his car and drove to the school to get Jack. They barely made it back to Josheka Farm as the roads filled rapidly with snowdrifts.

The snowdrifts eventually reached 20 feet tall in some locations.

Sadly, 145 people perished in the Armistice Day Blizzard. The National Weather Service made many changes to improve its forecasts after the intensity of the Armistice Day Blizzard surprised it.

Readers, please stay safe—take all weather warnings seriously.

Chapter 5 – Cirrus Clouds

Cirrus clouds form in very cold air high in the sky.

Most clouds are made up of tiny water droplets. But cirrus clouds are made up of ice crystals.

The ice crystals in cirrus clouds make them look like feathers!

The strong winds that make "tails" on cirrus clouds show the wind's direction. Cirrus clouds often travel from west to east.

Cirrus clouds usually occur when the weather is beautiful. Their appearance often means the weather is about to change for the worse.

Cirrus clouds often come before precipitation, such as rain. The ice crystals in cirrus clouds change back to a mist before hitting the ground.

Take a minute today to see if you can spot any cirrus clouds in the sky where you live!

Chapter 6 – Cumulus Clouds

The typical cumulus cloud weighs over 1 million pounds. That is the same as 100 elephants!

As air, warmed by the earth, rises, moisture in the air cools and turns into very tiny water drops. The water droplets gather as they rise and create the white, fluffy clouds we call cumulus.

Some clouds, such as cirrus clouds, are very high in the sky. Cumulus clouds are low in the sky. They often form below 6,500 feet of altitude.

The word "cumulus" comes from the Latin word for "heap" or "pile." Cumulus clouds often look a pile of cotton balls.

Cumulus clouds can form in lines which stretch over 300 miles. These are called cloud sheets, even when there are gaps in the sheets.

On most days, cumulus clouds don't produce rain. If conditions are right, they can change into rain-bearing clouds.

Chapter 7 – Dust Devils

Dust devils are a type of whirlwind!

They can be small, about 18 inches wide and just nine feet tall. Large dust devils can be more than 30 feet wide, and more than 3,000 feet tall.

Dust devils are generally harmless. But they can grow big enough to be a threat to people and property.

Similar to tornadoes, dust devils begin as a swirling updraft of air under sunny and nice weather. They are made when hot air rises fast inside a pocket of cooler air.

When the conditions are right, the wind starts to rotate. When the air rises, the dust devil starts to spin faster. As more air rushes in to replace the rising air, the spinning becomes even faster.

As the dust devil spins, the air pours out of the top. The air falls down the outside of the dust devil, and is sucked back into the center. The air will keep rising and falling like this with the right conditions.

Chapter 8 – Flooding

A major storm with steady rain causes flooding. Floods may also happen when dams break. In the winter, floods can happen when ice or snow melt fast.

Meteorologists define floods as water covering land which is usually dry.

The Great Flood of 1844 is thought to be the biggest flood in the world. It happened on the

Missouri River and the upper Missippi River in a region where few people lived at the time, so there wasn't as much destruction as later floods. The flood was the highest recorded for St. Louis, Missouri. Due to this flood, Congress passed the Swamp Act in 1849 to build ridges or walls along rivers and coastlines to control water levels.

Minor flooding happens when there is minimal property damage. Major flooding means extensive destruction of buildings and large evacuations of people and animals.

Chapter 9 – Hail

Hail is water which got caught in strong winds moving upward. The water vapor in the wind freezes, and then begins to fall as a ball of ice or hail. As the hailstone falls, it gathers more water and the hailstone grows. When the hailstone is too heavy for the winds to keep it in the air, it falls to the ground.

Most hailstones are small, but some hailstones can be as large as softballs. The stronger the updraft, the larger the hail stone.

When they begin falling, hailstones can fall as fast as 90 miles per hour. Small hailstones melt before hitting the earth. Larger hailstones can hit the earth. These large hailstones can cause damage to cars, awnings, and other objects.

Hail is common in mid-latitudes during the summer. That is when surface temperatures are warm, but the upper air is still cold. That is why hail can happen in the summertime.

Chapter 10 – Hurricane

A hurricane is a large tropical storm system with high-powered circular winds. A hurricane must have sustained winds of at least 74 miles per hour.

Meteorologists give hurricanes a 1 to 5 rating, called a category. This rating is based on a hurricane's maximum sustained winds.

"Hurricane Season" begins on June 1 and ends on November 30. But hurricanes can occur outside this window.

Cats, make sure your people have a hurricane preparedness plan that includes you! This means: obtain extra cat food, store enough water for all the cats, locate evacuation shelters that allow cats, keep cat carriers ready to go, and store plenty of cat supplies in the safe room.

Chapter 11 – Ice

From 212 degrees Fahrenheit to around 32 degrees Fahrenheit, water molecules are liquid.

Above 212 degrees Fahrenheit, water molecules form a gas called steam.

Below 32 degrees Fahrenheit, water molecules form a solid called ice.

Since ice crystals take up more space than liquid water, ice is not as dense and can float in liquid water. Ice has 15 different crystal forms.

Ice builds up when super-cold rain freezes on contact with surfaces that are colder than 32 degrees Farenheit. These surfaces can be the ground, trees, cars, and other objects.

Ice can be very dangerous to buildings, vehicles, trees, people, and animals. Roads and sidewalks become slippery. Tree branches can become so heavy with ice that they break off.

An ice storm that hit Maine, Massachusetts, and New Hampshire in December 2008 left millions of homes and businesses without electrical power. A state of emergency was declared.

But if you practice safety by dressing in warm layers, playing on ice in your backyard can be a lot of fun!

Chapter 12 – Rain

Rain is good for the planet. It gives us fresh water to drink ,and helps farmers grow crops. Everything is green and lush after a rain. Without rain, most of our planet would be a desert.

Water is always moving. The rain which falls on you today may have been in the ocean a few days ago.

As water vapor rises and cools, tiny drops of water are formed. As the droplets gather together, they get too heavy to stay in the air and fall to earth as rain.

Water may be in the sky, on land, in the ocean, and even underground. Water gets recycled many times, and this is called the "water cycle."

The highest amount of rainfall in one year was 1,000 inches in Cherrapunji, India between August 1, 1860 and July 31, 1861!

Chapter 13 – Rainbow

What is a rainbow?

Sunlight is made of different colors we don't normally see. When a sunbeam reaches earth, the light looks white.

Rainbows appear when sunlight and rain

blend. The sunlight beams separate, or divide, and we see the colors as each enters a raindrop.

As the sun passes through the raindrops at different speeds, the angle of each color is different. Depending on the angle, the color we see could be red, orange, yellow, green, blue, indigo, or violet. When all of these colors are mixed, we see white light.

The shape gives the rainbow its name. It's shaped like a bow used for shooting arrows. In ancient times, some people believed rainbows were used by a god of storms to shoot arrows of lightning!

Chapter 14 – Sleet

Sleet consists of ice pellets, often mixed with rain or snow. The raindrops may freeze as they fall. Typically, the snowflakes are not light and fluffy.

Don't confuse sleet with hail. Hail falls and rises many times before it falls to earth. Sleet falls only once.

How does sleet form? Think of a "warm-air sandwich" in the sky.

Precipitation begins as snow in the top, colder layer of air. The snow melts to form rain when falling through the warm layer. Rain re-freezes to form sleet in the bottom cold air near the ground.

Sleet can accumulate like snow, and create a hazard for walking and driving. Winter Storm Stella dropped a lot of sleet in the northeastern states of the United States in March 2017.

Sleet and hail form at different times of the year. Sleet forms in winter storms. While hail is also frozen precipitation, it forms during thunderstorms in the spring, summer, or fall.

A variety of wintry mixes can occur in the same storm – sleet, freezing rain, and snow. Personally, I think wintry mixes are super interesting!

Chapter 15 – Snow

Snow, like rain, hail, and sleet, is precipitation. Snow forms when the outside temperature reaches freezing or 32 degrees Farenheit.

Snow occurs when damp air forms ice crystals, skipping the rain step.

So snow can only form in really cold clouds. The temperature in the tops of the clouds needs to be around 20 degrees Fahrenheit.

All snowflakes have six sides. When a flake falls through a cloud, wet air will freeze on each side. Since no two snowflakes take the same path to the ground, each supposedly looks different.

There is a saying that no two snowflakes are alike. However, scientists cannot say for sure that no two snowflakes are alike as the snowflakes thaw too fast for accurate measurements!

Chapter 16 – Straight Line Winds

The damage these winds cause can be significant. Damage from straight line winds is more common than damage from tornadoes!

The source for straight line winds begins with a thunderstorm's downdraft.

As a thunderstorm's downdraft hits the surface

of the earth, it starts to roll. Think of a boat moving through water, leaving ripples behind it.

While the air rolls, it is squeezed or compressed. This often makes straight line winds increase faster than the winds inside a tornado.

The difference between straight line winds and a tornado can be summarized in two words: IN and OUT. Wind flows IN to a tornado. Wind flows OUT from straight line winds.

Straight line winds can break windows if the wind is faster than 200 miles per hour!

Chapter 17 – Stratus Clouds

Stratus clouds are thick and large. They dominate the sky. They are made of water and sometimes ice crystals. If you fly through a stratus cloud, there won't be many air bumps or much air turbulence. It will be difficult to see through them.

When stratus clouds are on the ground—or

very close— they are called fog. They can stop airplanes from taking off or landing.

Stratus clouds come in two types: 1) strato-cumulus, and 2) strato-nimbus.

Strato-cumulus cloud may cover the whole sky and are puffy. Strato-cumulus clouds appear when it has been cold outside, and warmer and wetter air moves in. While the warm air moves over the cold ground, water vapor is made. The water vapor then turns into drops of water which can form rain when the air is warm.

A strato-nimbus cloud is a stratus cloud which is making rain.

Chapter 18 – Sun Dogs

A sun dog is not a confused dog howling at the sun. It's not a dog at all – thank goodness!

A sun dog is a bright spot on the halo around the sun. It's made from the reflection of sunlight by small ice crystals in the air.

Often, two sun dogs on opposite sides of the sun can be seen.

Sun dogs usually appear at sunrise or sunset, but can appear any time during the day.

Sun dogs can be different colors. The colors depend on the way light reflects through the ice. The color of a sun dog is also determined by the distance from the sun. Usually, sun dogs have red inside edges. But sun dogs can be a bluish white when the distance from the sun is greater.

A sun dog's shape can change depending on the shape of ice crystals in the air. The ice crystals are made up of six triangular sides, but sometimes they are flat and long in shape. Such flat and long ice crystals create bright sun dogs.

Chapter 19 – Thundersnow

Thundersnow occurs when thunder and lightning happen during a snowstorm. This typically happens in late winter or early spring when a mass of cold air lies on top of warm air.

Moist air nearer the ground means thundersnow begins like a summer thunderstorm. The warmth of the sun heats the ground.

The warmer ground pushes piles of warm air upward and unstable air columns are made. The rising air starts to form clouds, and turbulence inside the new clouds starts to build.

For thundersnow to happen, the air near to the ground has to be warmer than the air above. The air near the earth still needs to be cold enough to create snow.

When thundersnow occurs, you can look for heavy snowfall. Two inches of snow an hour are possible!

In The *Adventure of the New Businesses*, I seeded the clouds and caused thundersnow for my weather blog business – which was totally and completely awesome! Unfortunately, my Uncle Ferd wasn't too happy about it.

Chapter 20 – Tornadoes

A tornado is a fast-spinning pillar of air reaching from a thunderstorm to the ground.

The most violent tornadoess can have wind speeds up to 300 miles per hour. Large buildings and trees can be destroyed. Cars and trucks can be thrown several times the length of a football field. Some tornadoes have thrown straw into trees with such force that the pieces of straw left holes in the trees!

A tornado's path can be more than one mile wide and 50 miles long.

In the United States, over 1,000 tornadoes occur every year.

Tornadoes usually come from thunderstorms. When warm, humid air from the Gulf of Mexico meets cool, dry air from Canada, the atmosphere is turbulent. As the wind changes direction, an invisible spinning starts. Most violent and strong tornadoes appear within this area of rapid spinning.

On the evening of May 5, 1965, the history of Laughing Thunder County records that an F4 tornado went right by my home at Josheka Farm. F4 tornadoes have wind speed of 207-260 miles per hour. This tornado caused damage along an 80-mile path. Seven people were injured by the tornado.

Thankfully, my cat ancestors had sensed the

change in barometric pressure, and fled to safety. Sailors have known of the weather sensing abilities of cats since the 1600s. They kept cats aboard their ships for weather predictions.

Part of the United States is called Tornado Alley. The heart of Tornado Alley includes Oklahoma, Texas, Kansas, Nebraska, Colorado, and South Dakota. Other states that may be impacted by tornadoes are Louisiana, Arkansas, Wyoming, North Dakota, Minnesota, Wisconsin, Iowa, Illinois, Indiana, Ohio, Tennessee, and Kentucky.

For safety, you should know the difference between a tornado watch and a tornado warning.

A tornado watch means that the potential exists for the development of severe thunderstorms or tornadoes. While no immediate action is required, you should monitor the weather situation and be prepared to seek shelter.

A tornado warning requires immediate action – head for shelter! A warning means that severe weather is imminent in your area or is already occurring. When a warning is issued, it means that a tornado has been either spotted by a human observer or indicated by Doppler radar. (Doppler radar uses microwave signals to measure the speed of tornadoes and other things.)

Fritz's Weather Activity –

The Weather Tracker

PLEASE HAVE AN ADULT HELP YOU!

- Materials:

- Notebook paper

- Pencil

- Outdoor thermometer

- Rain gauge

- Ruler

Directions:

Down the left side of a piece of notebook paper, write the seven days of the week: Monday, Tuesday, Wednesday, Thursday, Friday, Saturday, and Sunday.

Along the top of the paper write the following headings: Temperature, Sun, Precipitation, Clouds, Wind.

At the same time each day, record the temperature that you read from the outdoor thermometer under the Temperature heading.

Under the Sun heading, draw a sun if the sun is shining, or a cloud if it is cloudy. If the weather that day is half-sunny and half-cloudy, then draw a sun that is half-covered by a cloud.

Under the Precipitation heading, record the amount of precipitation measured by the rain gauge since your last measurement (empty the rain gauge after you read the measurement each day). If it is winter, then instead use a ruler to measure how much new snow has fallen since the day before.

Under the Clouds heading, record the type of clouds you see using the NWS Cloud Chart found at https://www.weather.gov/jetstream/cloudchart.

Finally, record your observation of the level

of wind using the Beaufort Wind Scale found at http://www.spc.noaa.gov/faq/tornado/beaufort.html.

Now you're a meteorologist just like me!

Also by S. S. Curtis:

The Cats of Laughing Thunder
in The New Businesses Adventure

The Cats of Laughing Thunder
in The Nasty Gray Adventure

The Cats of Laughing Thunder Guide
For Kids Starting A Business

Coming soon:

The Cats of Laughing Thunder
in The Moaning House Adventure

The Cats of Laughing Thunder
in The Scottish Invasion Adventure

The Cats of Laughing Thunder:
Sven's Viking Favorites

Excerpt from The Cats of Laughing Thunder in The New Businesses Adventure – Chapter 5:

Fritz's Weather Blog

Wednesday, March 15:

Weather Forecast for Josheka Farm, Laughing Thunder County, Minnesota - Mostly clear but cooler with a high of 32 degrees Fahrenheit

Fritz, Pumpkin, Sven, and Yolanda met the following morning.

"Thank the Great Cat it's teacher-in-service day, so we don't have Cat School," said Fritz. "My blimp's arrived and I need your help."

"What are we going to do?" asked Pumpkin.

"There's an ice jam on the Upper Lower

River," said Fritz. "I need to make a video of it for my website."

The cats climbed aboard the blimp.

"Ready for takeoff!" said Fritz.

Up the blimp went.

"Yolanda, help me with the weather instruments. Sven, steer the blimp. Pumpkin, shoot video," said Fritz.

Soon they were over the Upper Lower River.

"Wow, look at the flooding upstream!" said Fritz. "Look at the huge chunks of ice on the river banks!"

The cats gazed out the windows at the sight. The ice chunks were at least eight feet tall.

"It's the Ice Age again!" said Pumpkin.

Sven was so busy looking at the ice that he forgot to steer.

Crunch! Crash! Scrape!

The cats were thrown out of their seats, but Pumpkin managed to keep his camera recording. Fritz pushed himself off the floor. He had a barometer hanging around one ear.

"By the Great Cat, what happened?" asked Fritz.

The cats peered out the windows.

"We appear to be stuck in a giant oak tree," said Yolanda.

Fritz grabbed the controls. He pushed the control stick forward. He pushed the control stick backward. He did this three times.

Finally, the blimp pulled free from the tree.

"Sven, your time as pilot is over. I'll fly us home," Fritz said.

Excerpt from The Cats of Laughing

Thunder in The Nasty Gray

Adventure – Chapter 2:

Pumpkin and his friends were gathered outside after the meeting.

"I think we should help with the defense of our territory," said Pumpkin.

"But how?" said Yolanda, a cat with tuxedo markings. "Mayoress BT didn't assign any of us to patrol duty. She probably thinks we're too young to be useful. Even though we'd be way more useful than my pest of a big brother Yosh."

"We need to fight the enemy in every way possible," replied Pumpkin.

"I could use my weather blimp to spy on that

Nasty Gray and his minions," said Fritz, running a paw through his already tousled gray fur.

"Excellent idea," said Pumpkin.

"I know my mother would want me to help in the defense of our territory," said Sven. "Hmmm, remember class last month, when we were studying the Middle Ages? That has caused me to think about building a trebuchet."

Fritz frowned. "How does that apply here?" he asked.

"I could fill socks with rocks, and then launch them at the enemy with the trebuchet," said Sven.

"Great idea!" said Pumpkin.

Sven looked down modestly and groomed his brown tabby fur.

"What about you, Pumpkin?" asked Yolanda.

"I've invented a new martial art," said Pumpkin.

"By the Great Cat, what is it?" asked Fritz.

"I strap metal spikes to my tail, then lash my

tail about in combination with tae kwon do kicks," said Pumpkin.

"That sounds super cool! Will you teach us?" said Fritz.

"Sure, let's meet in the hillside pasture after Cat School," said Pumpkin.

That afternoon, Pumpkin strapped spikes on each cat's tail. Soon he had them sparring.

Pumpkin's grandmother discovered them training, and joined in.

About the Author

S. S. Curtis is the author of the Cats of Laughing Thunder series of fiction and non-fiction books for children. She grew up on a farm shared with a peak population of fifty-four cats of every color, shape, size, and personality imaginable. When S. S. Curtis had a child of her own, the cat population expanded with the addition of toy cats. All of those cats are her inspiration for the Cats of Laughing Thunder.

S. S. Curtis's father started her in business when she was five years old by giving her a beef calf to raise. Her next business venture was raising baby pigs with her brother. On the side, she did a little babysitting. After earning B.A., M.B.A., and J.D. degrees, she worked in the fields of consumer goods, law, and technology. She was a co-founder of ThinkerBlox,

LLC. Her child started an ornament business at the age of five, and is now a student at MIT pursuing business adventures in robotics.

You can explore the world of Laughing Thunder at http://www.laughingthunder.com and https://shop.laughingthunder.com.

www.ingramcontent.com/pod-product-compliance
Lightning Source LLC
Chambersburg PA
CBHW071637040426
42452CB00009B/1672